Developing Friendship WITH GOD

KENNETH COPELAND

FOUNDATION 6 STUDY GUIDE

Developing Friendship WITH GOD

KENNETH COPELAND

KENNETH
COPELAND
PUBLICATIONS

Developing Friendship With God
Study Guide

ISBN-10 1-57562-682-9 30-0723
ISBN-13 978-1-57562-682-6

23 22 21 20 19 18 9 8 7 6 5 4

Kenneth Copeland Publications
Fort Worth, TX 76192-0001

For more information about Kenneth Copeland Ministries, visit kcm.org or call 1-800-600-7395 (U.S. only) or +1-817-852-6000.

"Again, the kingdom of heaven is like unto treasure hid in a field; the which when a man hath found, he hideth, and for joy thereof goeth and selleth all that he hath, and buyeth that field."

Matthew 13:44

God gave all He had to purchase us…
His special treasure.

CD ONE

Developing Friendship With God

You Are God's Treasure!

"Again, the kingdom of heaven
is like unto treasure hid in a field; the which
when a man hath found, he hideth, and for joy
thereof goeth and selleth all
that he hath, and buyeth that field."
Matthew 13:44

You Are Precious to God, and He Wants to Have Fellowship With You

FOCUS: "The world is the field…" (Matthew 13:38). That's us. We're God's treasure!

Do you know that you are precious to God, and He wants to have fellowship with you? It's true. No matter who you are or what you have done, you're still a treasure to God. So much so, He gave all He had to purchase you.

In Matthew 13, God called the world—the human race—a treasure before it was fit to pay the price for. But He went ahead and sold all He had to get it. How could He look at a totally ungodly, compromised, treasonous earth, and mankind that literally belonged to the devil, and call it a treasure?

Romans 4:17 provides the amazing answer. It says God calls things that be not as though they were. He doesn't look at things the way they are. He looks at them the way they are going to be when He gets through with them.

In other words, God operates totally and completely *by faith.* He is so much a faith being that it's impossible to please Him without it.

The Bible also says the new birth, the plan of redemption, was *hidden in God* from the foundation of the world.

> God gave all He had to purchase you.

Mark 16 says that after His resurrection, Jesus appeared to Mary Magdalene. When she told the disciples she had seen Him, they didn't believe her. Later, Jesus upbraided, or reproved them because of their unbelief—because they weren't operating in faith. In John 20:27, He told Thomas, "Be not faithless, but believing."

Jesus stuck His neck out far enough to buy and pay for the earth with His own blood and get it all back, not knowing if one human being would ever believe it. He spoke by faith, calling things that be not as though they were. He looked through the eye of faith and said, "My house will be full" (see Luke 14:23).

God never changes. He never speaks darkness, death or defeat. He always speaks life. He speaks The Word that is full of light, healing, power and love. He speaks belief. He believed enough to give all He had, without reserve.

Rise Up to the Level of Confidence God Has in You

FOCUS: The truth is, "the gospel of Christ…is the power of God unto salvation to every one that believeth…" (Romans 1:16). When someone believes it, the saving, healing, delivering power of God will come.

When you find a treasure in The Word, God expects you to do as the man did who found a treasure in the field. *He sold all he had and depended on that treasure to put him over.* You're no longer just depending on things in the natural. You're standing and depending on the truth of The Word.

You may wonder if you have enough confidence. Hebrews 10:35-36 says you do: "Cast not away therefore your confidence, which hath great recompence of reward. For ye have need of patience, that, after ye have done the will of God, ye might receive the promise." The spiritual confidence God has given you is the very root of boldness—and it is the key to receiving the treasure you find promised in The Word.

The scripture we read in Hebrews 10 talks about confidence, patience and promise, which is the will of God. They all work together. With patience, you can stand on The Word until you see the promise.

You may want to see things change instantly, but God normally works through seedtime and harvest. The Word says the whole kingdom of God is as a seed planted in a field. That's the way God does everything—with seed—continuously.

Faith works the same way. If you'll plant it as a seed, it will grow.

When Jesus' own disciples asked Him to, "Increase our faith" (Luke 17:5), He answered them, "If ye have faith as a grain of mustard seed, ye shall say…" (Matthew 17:20). Or in other words, plant what you have and it will grow. That's the way God does things.

God looks at things the way they are going to be when He gets through with them.

There are four things that can help you develop God's kind of confidence:

1. Prayer
2. Fellowship with God—becoming a friend of God
3. Constant meditation in The Word
4. Continual praise

What most people call prayer isn't really prayer at all. There are prayers that can actually destroy confidence in God. Like when someone just rehearses the problem, talking about it over and over. The fact is, what you hear yourself saying is critical to either building or destroying your faith.

Just look at what Mark 11:22-23 says: "Have faith in God. For verily I say unto you, That whosoever shall say unto this mountain, Be thou removed, and be thou cast into the sea; and shall not doubt in his heart, but shall believe that those things which he saith shall come to pass; he shall have whatsoever he saith."

The highest form of prayer that exists is bringing God's Word back to Him with praise. It's not approaching God on the basis of your need. Always approach Him on the basis of the *provision* He has already made for your needs. When you continually speak of the need, you give it eternal status. Instead, praise and thank God for His Word and His provision.

Go to His Word that guarantees the answer, and just as He does, begin to call things that be not as though they were. Just say what God has said, and thank Him that your needs are met according to His riches in glory by Christ Jesus (Philippians 4:19).

Real praise is when you begin thanking God because you call things that be not as though they *were.* The Bible says God perfects the praise of our lips and He inhabits our praise. He's right there in it with you, but He's not the One who needs to hear it. You are. As you say it and hear it all day long, your spirit man begins to rise up and take hold of it.

When you hear yourself say it enough times, your confidence begins to grow and you become bolder and bolder. You've been feeding your spirit, and now out of the abundance of your heart, your mouth is about to speak. Without even having to think about it, because your faith has grown, this is when the power comes out of your spirit.

Real prayer and praise will move you into the area of true fellowship with God. For instance, look at how Jesus spoke at the tomb of Lazarus: "Father, I thank thee that thou hast heard me. And I knew that thou hearest me always: but because of the people which stand by I said it, that they may believe that thou hast sent me. And when he thus had spoken, he cried with a loud voice, Lazarus, come forth" (John 11:41-43). That's straight talk, isn't it? He was saying, I know You already heard Me.

When did God hear Him? Four days earlier when He said, "This sickness is not unto death…" (John 11:4). Jesus called things that be not as though they were and then He continued in faith until they were.

You may be calling things that be not as though they were. Now begin to give God thanksgiving for it. Let all of heaven know you and God are in agreement over this!

When you find treasure in The Word, and move on what God says, you can fully expect it to come to pass!

Second Corinthians 4:18 says, "We look not at the things which are seen, but at the things which are not seen: for the things which are seen are temporal [temporary]; but the things which are not seen are eternal."

The Bible says the things you can see are only temporary. If you can see it, it's subject to change. But if you continue to call things that are as they are, they'll never change. You just give them eternal status.

Now Begin Enjoying It

Begin to call things that be not as though they were. First Corinthians 1:28 says God has chosen "things which are not, to bring to nought things that are." You can change the things that are bothering you.

CD 1 Outlined

I. God called the world—the human race—a treasure before it was worth paying for
  A. The field is the world (Matthew 13:36)
  B. God paid all He had to purchase it (Matthew 13:44-46)
  C. He did it by faith
    1. God operates by faith; He is a faith being
    2. God calls things that be not as though they were (Romans 4:17)

II. The plan of redemption was hidden in God from the foundation of the world
  A. Only God and Jesus understood it

III. God believed enough to give all He had
  A. God has complete confidence in His own Word
  B. If you truly believe, you will be totally committed and *do* what you believe
  C. Four things that develop God's kind of confidence in The Word
    1. Prayer
    2. Fellowship with God—becoming a friend of God
    3. Constant meditation in The Word
    4. Continual praise

Study Questions

(1) When God paid the ultimate price for the world, what condition was it in?

(2) How could He be sure it would be worth the price He had to pay?

(3) What is God's method of operation?

(4) How does God see the human race, including the unregenerated world?

(5) What four spiritual activities help you develop God's kind of confidence in The Word?

Study Notes

"Go out into the highways and hedges, and compel them to come in, that my house may be filled."
Luke 14:23

"For God so loved the world, that he gave his only begotten Son...."

John 3:16

God loves you...
He wants to have fellowship with you...
He wants to be your friend.

CD TWO

Become a Friend of God

"[God] hath raised us up together, and made us sit together in heavenly places in Christ Jesus: that in the ages to come he might show the exceeding riches of his grace in his kindness toward us through Christ Jesus."
Ephesians 2:6-7

God loves you...He is rich in mercy. And He wants to have fellowship with you!

While We Were Yet in Sin, God Loved Us

FOCUS: "But God!... Because of and in order to satisfy the great and wonderful and intense love with which He loved us, even when we were dead (slain) by [our own] shortcomings and trespasses, He made us alive together in fellowship and in union with Christ" (Ephesians 2:4-5, *The Amplified Bible).*

God loves you and wants to be your friend. Over and over, the Bible attests to the fact that God's love for mankind is unwavering. As we have already seen, even when man was in a fallen state, totally separated from God, He was calling us His treasure. From John 3:16 to Ephesians 2, we see God sending His Son to purchase His treasure—redeeming His fellowship with man. But we have accused Him of all kinds of destructive and negative acts because of a lack of knowledge and understanding of what He is like. Mankind has blamed God for all kinds of murder and destruction because of a misunderstanding of death, as well as a misunderstanding of man's authority in the earth.

God does not murder. He is not the taker of life; He's the giver of life. So the only places in the Bible where you see God taking life is in defense of His people. But He judges it a righteous thing to vindicate and defend His own people.

> *God loves you and He wants to be your friend.*

In fact, God loves us so much, He sent Jesus to deliver us from the power of death. Until Jesus came, the devil had the power of death. But because of Jesus' sacrifice, we have been delivered from him who had the power of death (Hebrews 2:14). Now, through Jesus, we have authority and a choice in the matter.

In Philippians 1:21-25, the Apostle Paul said that he couldn't decide whether to stay in his body or go home to be with Jesus. It was his choice.

Although we have a choice, it's not God's will for anyone to die younger than 70 (Psalm 90:10).

According to Proverbs 18:21, "Death and life are in the power of the tongue." But because of lack of knowledge and understanding of this, Christians can die needlessly. Hosea 4:6 says, "My people are destroyed for lack of knowledge." They can also die as a result of not rightly discerning the body and blood of Jesus (1 Corinthians 11:27-30). The proper death for believers would be to live until their job on earth is completely finished and then depart, not be evicted from their bodies.

That's what Jesus did. He said that He could take up or lay down His own life; no one could take it from Him (John 10:17-18).

Begin to Develop Friendship and Fellowship With Him

FOCUS: "Beloved, if our heart condemn us not, then have we confidence toward God. And whatsoever we ask, we receive of him, because we keep his commandments, and do those things that are pleasing in his sight" (1 John 3:21-22).

One thing believers need to do is develop a boldness or confidence in the gospel. This passage in 1 John 3 makes it clear that having a heart that doesn't condemn you is a critical factor in this process.

If your heart is condemning you about something, deal with it. Get to the root of the problem. Go back to the last thing God told you to do and do it. You will then begin to receive revelation and grow in The Word again.

Also, start acting in love. It's the commandment of the Church. Don't try to change everyone else—change yourself.

Now, let's talk about two vitally important spiritual activities that are part of your relationship with God—prayer and fellowship. They blend together. There is no such thing as prayer without fellowshiping with God, and there's no such thing as fellowshiping with God without prayer. Your confidence affects both of them.

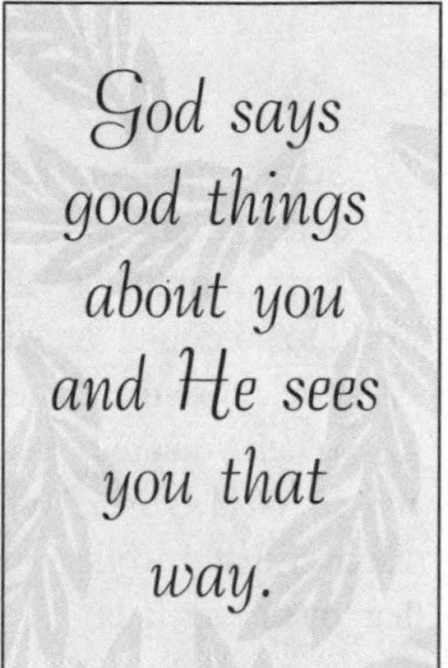
God says good things about you and He sees you that way.

Also, developing fellowship with God is literally developing a friendship with Him. We see an example of this in the Bible when Abraham was called the friend of God (see 2 Chronicles 20:7; Isaiah 41:8). He qualified for that title because he put action to his faith: "Abraham believed God, and it was imputed unto him for righteousness: and he was called the Friend of God. Ye see then how that by works a man is justified, and not by faith only" (James 2:23).

The Hebrew word translated *friend* is a very deep word for love and intercommunication between people. That's what God wants from us. In fact, He is more eager for friendship with us than we are.

Being a friend of God is a very high calling. It takes time and effort to develop. But you don't develop that friendship, or any other, by acting just any way you want. You guard the way you act because you don't want to offend the Father and you don't want to offend Jesus. You'll find that this will do more to get sin out of your life than anything else.

Now Begin Enjoying It

Start seeing yourself as God sees you. No matter what you may have been in the past, God says good things about you and He sees you that way.

First Corinthians 1:27 says, "God hath chosen the foolish things of the world to confound the wise...." Remember, God originally chose sinners. But since He chose them, they didn't remain foolish, and neither do you.

When you are born again, you become His child, a joint heir with Jesus. *You are God's friend.* When you walk continually in the love of God, you'll discover that it works in your own life. In all your friendships, you'll discover that love never fails.

CD 2 Outlined

I. God called mankind a treasure before He paid the price for it
   A. He sold all He had and bought it (Matthew 13:37-46)
   B. "For God so loved the world, that he gave his only begotten Son..." (John 3:16)
      1. While we were yet in sin, God loved us (Ephesians 2:4-5)
   C. God's commandments are a true picture of Him

II. Man has misunderstood death and his own authority on the earth
   A. God is the giver of life, not the taker
   B. Through Jesus, we have authority and a choice
      1. "Death and life are in the power of the tongue" (Proverbs 18:21)

III. We can operate like God
   A. We have been born again of His Spirit and in His likeness
   B. Call things that be not as though they were (Romans 4:17)

IV. Believers must develop confidence or boldness in the gospel

V. Developing fellowship with God is literally developing a friendship with God
   A. The Hebrew word translated *friend* is a very deep word for love and intercommunication

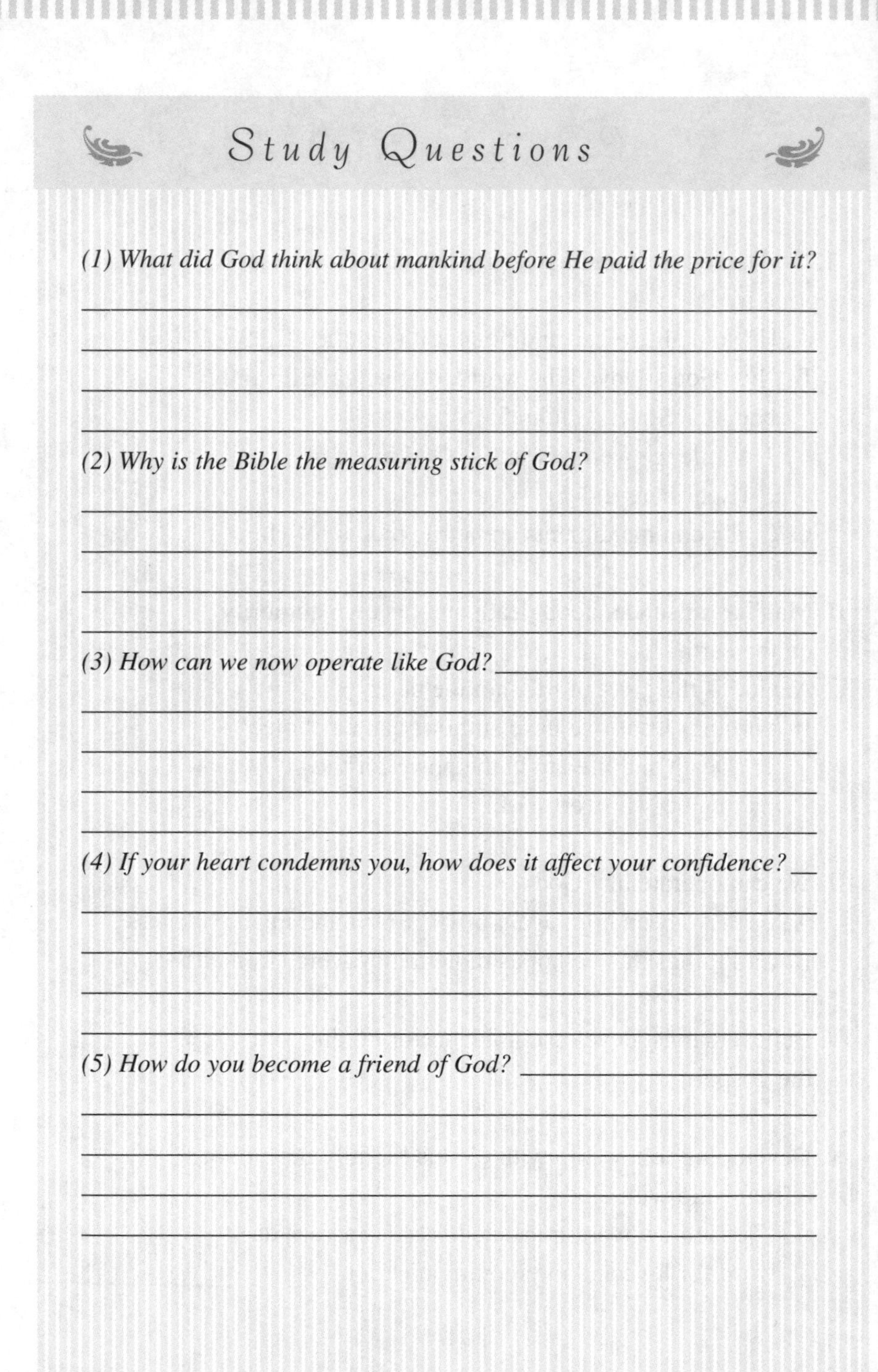

Study Questions

(1) What did God think about mankind before He paid the price for it?

(2) Why is the Bible the measuring stick of God?

(3) How can we now operate like God?

(4) If your heart condemns you, how does it affect your confidence?

(5) How do you become a friend of God?

Study Notes

"He answered and said unto them, He that soweth the good seed is the Son of man."
Matthew 13:37

"God. . .calleth those things which be not as though they were."

Romans 4:17

God called mankind His treasure…
when there was not one righteous. He saw
us through the eye of faith.We can have His
kind of faith, love and confidence.

CD THREE

Become Sold Out to Faith and Love

"But without faith it is impossible to please [God]…."
Hebrews 11:6

You Can Have the God Kind of Confidence

FOCUS: "Again, the kingdom of heaven is like unto treasure hid in a field; the which when a man hath found, he hideth, and for joy thereof goeth and selleth all that he hath, and buyeth that field" (Matthew 13:44).

When God decided to redeem mankind, He was completely sold out—there was no turning back. And we can have that kind of faith and confidence in The Word, the things of God and the power of God to completely sell out like He did when He came after us.

There is a place of faith and confidence in God's Word where we can be completely sold out to the fact that God's Word works, so convinced of its truth, we'll lay everything on the line because of it.

That's like the man in Matthew 13 who found the treasure in the field. The Bible says he *hid* that treasure. He didn't go and tell everyone what he had found. He hid it until he could go and sell all he had to buy it.

When the man did that, everyone else probably thought he was crazy to sell everything he had and buy one piece of land, but they didn't understand what he knew. It takes a lot of faith to do what that man did. You see, he knew God told him to buy that field, and that it held a treasure he couldn't do without. But no one else understood that.

> God gave all He had to purchase you.

People thought Abraham, David and Moses were crazy too for doing what God said, but their stories prove that it pays to serve God, no matter what it looks like at the time.

Did you ever think about when Abraham offered Isaac on the altar, what Isaac's part of that was like? It took a lot of faith and confidence on Isaac's part…both in his father and in God.

Abraham had absolute confidence in God. He said, "God will provide..." (Genesis 22:8). It was because of that kind of confidence that Abraham was called the friend of God (see Isaiah 41:8; 2 Chronicles 20:7).

The Hebrew word translated *friend* in these scriptures is a word for a deep-running love and partnership between two people. It is literally holy in its context because it is so deep. It is a word that describes a relationship like Jonathan and David...people who would die for one another.

It's like the love Jesus had when He died for us. He hung on the Cross in our place. He went to hell in our place so we wouldn't have to go. He took the pains of sickness and disease that were meant for us. He took the chastisement of our peace—all the worry, mental agony and disease that were meant for us, Jesus bore so we wouldn't have to.

Jesus did all that for us because He loves us. He's our friend!

Now look what He said in John 15:7-10: "If ye abide in me, and my words abide in you, ye shall ask what ye will, and it shall be done unto you.... As the Father hath loved me, so have I loved you: continue ye in my love. *If ye keep my commandments, ye shall abide in my love;* even as I have kept my Father's commandments, and abide in his love."

Jesus was saying if we keep His commandments, we will take up residence in His love. We will never be without His love. He was talking about more than just His loving us enough to die for us. He was talking about walking and living and having our lifestyle in His love. He was talking about friendship—a fellowship—having Jesus as our best friend.

He said, "If ye keep My commandments, ye shall abide in my love, even as I have kept my Father's commandments, and abide in his love." There is great friendship between Jesus and the Father.

You can see this by the way Jesus acted. In John 8:28 He said, "I do nothing of myself; but as my Father hath taught me, I speak these things." Well, what did the Father say? He said, "I've turned everything over to the Son." (See John 5:22.)

Each points to the other. They're not taking for themselves. Both are giving to each other. That's the most beautiful picture of friendship there is.

That's why Jesus could say, "He that hath seen me hath seen the Father" (John 14:9).

Then in John 17:20-22, Jesus went on to say, "[Father, cause them to] be one...even as we are one." Jesus was talking about more than just attending a couple of church services on Sunday or a prayer meeting on Wednesday night. He was talking about a total commitment in thought, speech and every realm of life.

When you draw near to God. He will draw near to you.

Being committed and a friend of God is always to your advantage. For instance, Proverbs 18:24 says, "There is a friend that sticketh closer than a brother." A close friend will stay with you. That's the way God is and that's the way Jesus is. Hebrews 13:5 says, "I will never leave thee, nor forsake thee," and in Matthew 28:20, Jesus said, "Lo, I am with you always, even to the end of the age" *(New King James Version).*

What Qualifies You to Be Called Jesus' Friend?

FOCUS: "Ye are my friends, if ye do whatsoever I command you" (John 15:14).

In John 15:14, Jesus tells us what qualifies someone to be called His friend. He was saying, "If you'll do what I tell you to do, you can be My friend." Again, a perfect example of this is found in James 2:23, where we are told "Abraham believed God, and it was imputed unto him for righteousness: and he was called the Friend of God." Why? He put action to his faith. When he did that, his faith was completed and fulfilled, it was accounted unto him as righteousness, and God called him His friend.

In short, put action to your faith, and God the Father will call you His friend.

According to James 4:2-3: "Ye have not, because ye ask not. Ye ask, and receive not, because ye ask amiss, that ye may consume it upon your lusts." These are the two fundamental reasons why any born-again believer lacks anything in his life. He either didn't ask at all, or he asked and didn't receive it because he asked amiss.

When you don't align yourself with The Word, here's where asking amiss comes in: *that you may consume it upon your lusts*. That's the key to prosperity right there.

If you're going to consume God's things on your lusts, then God won't reveal to you the laws of prosperity to receive it. But when you develop confidence and ask correctly so that you receive, it brings a joy that Jesus talked about in John 16:24: "Ask, and ye shall receive, that your joy may be full."

In Mark 11:23, Jesus said you have what you say. No one is immune to this law. When you speak, it becomes the voice of authority in your life.

This is the way God operates all the time. He is totally committed to it. Everything He does, He does by calling things that be not as though they were. It's a complete and total commitment to faith. Even when He says, "For verily I say unto you..." He's using this method.

Friendship and fellowship with God is the richest thing God has ever made available to the human being. That's the reason He created us in His image. That's why He created us in His class of being. Now, through Jesus, we belong to a heavenly class.

God created us in His image. Then He re-created us in the likeness of Jesus. He brought us into His class because He wanted to fellowship with us.

Now Begin Enjoying It

Remember, Jesus said you shall have whatsoever you say. In verse 24, He went on to say, "Therefore I say unto you, What things soever ye desire, when ye pray, believe that ye receive them, and ye shall have them." Since Jesus said this, it has to work because Jesus has what He says. In the same way, what *I* say comes to pass—because I say what He said—and because I believe.

God wants to be your friend more than you can imagine. Start drawing near to Him, and He will draw near to you. Remember, He loves you...*just the way you are.*

CD 3 Outlined

I. When God decided to redeem mankind, He was completely sold out—there was no turning back

II. We can have God's kind of faith and confidence in The Word
   A. We can be completely sold out to the fact that The Word works
      1. Being so convinced it is true, we will lay everything on the line because of it
   B. Answer every circumstance by faith
   C. Take time to build confidence in God's Word
      1. Abraham had confidence in God
      2. Because of that confidence, Abraham was called the friend of God

III. The Hebrew word translated *friend* describes a deep-running love and partnership between two people

IV. Jesus said, "If ye keep my commandments, ye shall abide in my love" (John 15:10)
   A. This is a fellowship—a friendship—having Jesus as your best friend

V. There is great friendship between Jesus and the Father
   A. Each points to the other
   B. Both are giving to each other, not taking for themselves

VI. Jesus prayed, "[Father, that they may] be one even as we are one" (John 17:20-23)
   A. This is a total commitment in thought, speech, every realm of life

CD 3 Outlined

VII. Being committed to God, being friends with God, is always to your advantage
   A. "There is a friend that sticketh closer than a brother" (Proverbs 18:24)
   B. "I will never leave thee, nor forsake thee" (Hebrews 13:5)
   C. "Lo, I am with you always, even unto the end of the age" (Matthew 28:20, *New King James Version)*

VIII. In Jesus' opinion, what qualifies you to be called His friend?
   A. "Ye are my friends, if ye do whatsoever I command you" (John 15:14)
   B. Abraham was called the friend of God because he put action to his faith (James 2:21-23)

IX. Friendship and fellowship with God is the richest thing God has made available to the human being
   A. He created us in His image
   B. Now, through Jesus, we belong to a heavenly class of beings
   C. He brought us into His class because He wanted to fellowship with us

Study Questions

(1) How can we have God's kind of faith and confidence in The Word?

(2) In Jesus' opinion, what qualifies you to be called His friend?

(3) What will be the results of keeping God's commandments?

(4) What is the key to prosperity?

(5) What can you do to have God draw near to you?

Study Notes

"A man that hath friends must show himself friendly: and there is a friend that sticketh closer than a brother."
Proverbs 18:24

Study Notes

"Go out into the highways and hedges, and compel them to come in, that my house may be filled."
Luke 14:23

"But God hath chosen... things which are not, to bring to nought things that are."

1 Corinthians 1:27-28

"And God said, Let there be light: and there was light."

Genesis 1:3

God always calls things that be not as though they were. That's God's plan of dominion and authority for you, too.

CD FOUR

Let The Word Convert You

"By hearing ye shall hear, and shall not understand; and seeing ye shall see, and shall not perceive: for this people's heart is waxed gross, and their ears are dull of hearing, and their eyes they have closed; lest at any time they should see [the Word] with their eyes, and hear [the Word] with their ears, and should understand with their heart, and should be converted, and I should heal them."

Matthew 13:14-15, *author's paraphrase*

God Wants You to Be Part of His Plan of Dominion and Authority

FOCUS: "If thou seekest [wisdom] as silver, and searchest for her as for hid treasures; Then shalt thou understand the fear of the Lord, and find the knowledge of God" (Proverbs 2:4-5).

We have looked at Romans 4:17 and 1 Corinthians 1:27-28 in several different ways. What we want to see now is this: *Calling things that be not as though they were is God's plan of dominion and authority...and it's available to you.* That's the way God intends for all His people to exercise dominion in His Name.

Our spiritual vision is limited. But God can see things we can't. He wants us to start seeing like He sees...by faith.

A good example of this is found in 2 Kings 6, in the story of Elijah and his servant Gehazi. Gehazi, seeing the city surrounded by enemy forces, was alarmed. But Elisha began calling things that be not as though they were: "There are more of us than there are of them" (verse 16). Then when Elisha asked God to open Gehazi's eyes, his servant saw that they were surrounded by thousands of angels and chariots of fire. God's war machinery was lining those hills, just waiting for that old prophet to say the word. But he didn't have to see them. He was walking by faith...and so can you.

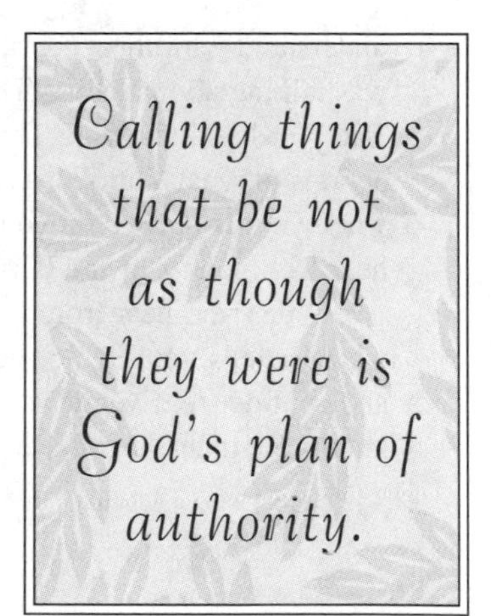
Calling things that be not as though they were is God's plan of authority.

Every one of us has angels assigned to us. Don't keep them bound up by calling things that are as though they are. Start calling things that be not as though they were—you do that by speaking spiritual words. What are spiritual words? The Word of God.

For instance, if you need healing, don't go around saying you are sick. Go to The Word and find scriptures like 1 Peter 2:24 and Isaiah 53:5 that say you are healed: "But he [Jesus] was wounded for our transgressions, he was bruised for our iniquities: the chastisement of our peace was upon him; and with his stripes we are healed."

If you want to be healed, talk healing—talk The Word. That's how you develop confidence like God has. You develop confidence in God's Word by meditation in it, by prayer and by developing fellowship with God, talking to Him all the time.

Whether you need healing, finances or anything else, the Bible is the greatest source of supply. That's why Proverbs says it is greater than the merchandise of silver or gold. But you have to build confidence to the point where it is that way in your life.

God wants us to start seeing like He does...by faith.

In Matthew 13, Jesus, talking about people who hear The Word but aren't changed by it, said, "lest at any time they should see with their eyes, and hear with their ears, and should understand with their heart, and should be converted..." (verse 15). He was talking about seeing The Word, hearing The Word, understanding The Word and allowing The Word to convert our minds, tongues and actions to what The Word says instead of the way things look. That's when God is able to move into our situations. That's when we begin to hear from God and see Him act on our behalf.

When you hear from God, you will then have confidence to act on what He tells you. Somewhere down the line, decide to move with faith and confidence. Even if you make a mistake, God can still use an act of faith more than He can use indecision and a lack of obedience.

Praise God With the Promises You Have Found in The Word

FOCUS: "God inhabits the praises of His people" (Psalm 22:3, author's paraphrase).

If you need healing, say something like this, "God, I praise You and worship You. It's so good to be up out of bed. It's so good not to have any pain. Thank You that by Jesus' stripes I am healed!"

Isaiah 57:19 says God creates the fruit of our lips, which, according to Hebrews 13:15, is the praise of Almighty God. "By him therefore let us offer the sacrifice of praise to God continually, that is, the fruit of our lips giving thanks to his name." Notice this says we are to praise Him *continually*. As priests of God (Revelation 1:6), we are actually ordained to make sacrifices of praise.

When you agree with The Word and praise Him for it, you'll see the results.

Not only that, Psalm 50:23 says, "Whoso offereth praise glorifieth me: and to him that ordereth his conversation aright will I show the salvation of God." Praise glorifies God, and when you praise Him, you bring Him on the scene.

We saw earlier that praise is the highest form of prayer that exists.

So when you bring together The Word of God, calling things that be not as though they were and praise, you'll begin to receive insight from The Word. With this vital combination, the moment God says something to you about The Word, *let it convert you.*

The Bible says God's promises are yea and amen (2 Corinthians 1:20). So any time you go to The Word and it says, "By His stripes you were healed," "My God shall supply all your needs according to His riches in glory by Christ Jesus," or whatever you need to receive, say "Yes! Amen!" When you agree with The Word and praise Him for it, you'll see the results.

Now, let's look at an incident in Jesus' life where praise was what

When you want to act in faith, go first to The Word.

made all the difference.

When Jesus was being crucified, Matthew 27:46 quotes Him as saying, "My God, my God, why hast thou forsaken me?" A few minutes later He also said, "It is finished" (John 19:30). He was quoting Psalm 22—all of it. Praise was the weapon He used to defeat hell and the grave. Praising God with the promise of His Word always brings Him on the scene.

God will do something with you if you will step out on His Word. If you won't, there's nothing He can do with you.

Praise is what defeated the devil and all of hell. Praise is what put the shackles on him. It's the sword Jesus used to kick open the gates of hell and take the keys of death. The devil had no keys left—he had been defeated.

Even when Jesus was on the cross, He was speaking The Word, calling things that be not as though they were, and praising God. It was a vital, winning combination that worked for Him, even in hell itself.

Now Begin Enjoying It

Listen in your spirit, and be ready to act on what God tells you, one step at a time. You see, God will cause you to walk by faith. He isn't going to spell out every detail for you in the beginning. As you begin to act by faith, your confidence will keep building and your faith stays on the line.

When you have a need and you want to act in faith, first of all, *go to The Word.* Find every promise that has to do with your situation. Then find every scripture about answered prayer. Take those scriptures, put them in your eyes and in your ears. Read them. Listen to faith tapes with scriptures about what you are believing for. Turn off everything else.

Like Jesus, make praise your lifestyle to live on The Word every day until it is what always comes out of your mouth. Continually call things that be not as though they were like God does, and continually praise Him that it's done. It worked for Jesus, it will work for you.

CD 4 Outlined

I. Calling things that be not as though they were is God's plan of dominion and authority
   A. It's available to you
   B. It's how God intends for all His people to exercise dominion and authority
      1. Speak the promises
      2. You will develop confidence like God has

II. Reach for The Word first as your source in every situation
   A. The Bible is the greatest source for whatever you need
   B. It is greater than the merchandise of silver or gold (Proverbs 3:13-15)

III. You can receive understanding from The Word of God
   A. By meditation, studying it, confessing it, acting on it
   B. Proverbs 4:7

IV. God will do something with you if you will step out on His Word

V. When you have a need and want to act in faith, first of all, go to The Word.
   A. Find every promise that applies to your situation
   B. Find every scripture about answered prayer
   C. Put those scriptures in your eyes and ears
   D. Turn off everything else

CD 4 Outlined

VI. Praise God with the promises you found in The Word
- A. God inhabits the praises of His people (Psalm 22:3)
- B. God creates the fruit of our lips (Isaiah 57:19)
- C. The fruit of our lips is the praise of Almighty God (Hebrews 13:15)
- D. We are priests of God, ordained to offer the sacrifice of praise continually
- E. Praise glorifies God and brings Him on the scene (Psalm 50:23)
- F. Praise is the highest form of prayer that exists

VII. Praise made all the difference when Jesus was crucified
- A. On the Cross, He was quoting Psalm 22
- B. He went into hell itself with the Psalms coming out of His mouth
- C. Praise was the weapon He used to defeat the devil and all of hell
- D. Jesus went into hell praising, and He praised until it raised Him up

VIII. Like Jesus, make it your lifestyle to live on The Word
- A. Let it be what always comes out of your mouth
- B. Continually call things that be not as though they were, like God does
- C. Continually praise God that it's done
- D. It will work for you right where you are now

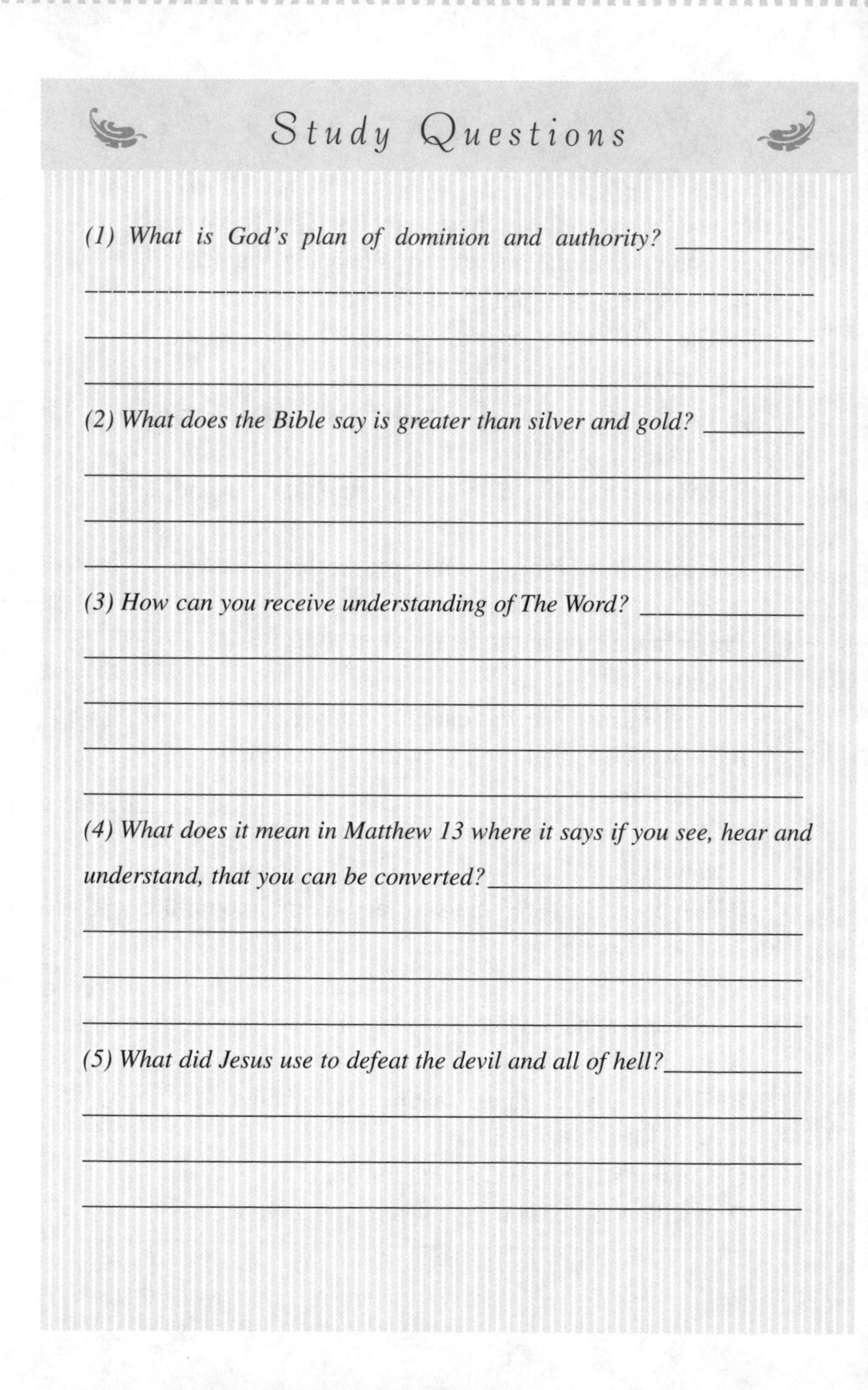

Study Questions

(1) What is God's plan of dominion and authority? ____________

(2) What does the Bible say is greater than silver and gold? ____________

(3) How can you receive understanding of The Word? ____________

(4) What does it mean in Matthew 13 where it says if you see, hear and understand, that you can be converted? ____________

(5) What did Jesus use to defeat the devil and all of hell? ____________

Study Notes

"Peace, peace to him that is far off, and to him that is near, saith the Lord; and I will heal him."
Isaiah 57:19

Prayer for Salvation and Baptism in the Holy Spirit

Heavenly Father, I come to You in the Name of Jesus. Your Word says, "Whosoever shall call on the name of the Lord shall be saved" (Acts 2:21). I am calling on You. I pray and ask Jesus to come into my heart and be Lord over my life according to Romans 10:9-10: "If thou shalt confess with thy mouth the Lord Jesus, and shalt believe in thine heart that God hath raised him from the dead, thou shalt be saved. For with the heart man believeth unto righteousness; and with the mouth confession is made unto salvation." I do that now. I confess that Jesus is Lord, and I believe in my heart that God raised Him from the dead. I repent of sin. I renounce it. I renounce the devil and everything he stands for. Jesus is my Lord.

I am now reborn! I am a Christian—a child of Almighty God! I am saved! You also said in Your Word, "If ye then, being evil, know how to give good gifts unto your children: HOW MUCH MORE shall your heavenly Father give the Holy Spirit to them that ask him?" (Luke 11:13). I'm also asking You to fill me with the Holy Spirit. Holy Spirit, rise up within me as I praise God. I fully expect to speak with other tongues as You give me the utterance (Acts 2:4). In Jesus' Name. Amen!

Begin to praise God for filling you with the Holy Spirit. Speak those words and syllables you receive—not in your own language, but the language given to you by the Holy Spirit. You have to use your own voice. God will not force you to speak. Don't be concerned with how it sounds. It is a heavenly language!

Continue with the blessing God has given you and pray in the spirit every day.

You are a born-again, Spirit-filled believer. You'll never be the same!

Find a good church that boldly preaches God's Word and obeys it. Become part of a church family who will love and care for you as you love and care for them.

We need to be connected to each other. It increases our strength in God. It's God's plan for us.

Make it a habit to watch the Believer's Voice of Victory Network and become a doer of the Word, who is blessed in his doing (James 1:22-25).

About the Author

Kenneth Copeland is co-founder and president of Kenneth Copeland Ministries in Fort Worth, Texas, and best-selling author of books that include *Honor—Walking in Honesty, Truth and Integrity,* and *THE BLESSING of The LORD Makes Rich and He Adds No Sorrow With It.*

Since 1967, Kenneth has been a minister of the gospel of Christ and teacher of God's Word. He is also the artist on award-winning albums such as his Grammy-nominated *Only the Redeemed, In His Presence, He Is Jehovah, Just a Closer Walk* and *Big Band Gospel.* He also co-stars as the character Wichita Slim in the children's adventure videos *The Gunslinger, Covenant Rider* and the movie *The Treasure of Eagle Mountain,* and as Daniel Lyon in the Commander Kellie and the Superkids™ videos *Armor of Light* and *Judgment: The Trial of Commander Kellie.* Kenneth also co-stars as a Hispanic godfather in the 2009 and 2016 movies *The Rally* and *The Rally 2: Breaking the Curse.*

With the help of offices and staff in the United States, Canada, England, Australia, South Africa and Ukraine, Kenneth is fulfilling his vision to boldly preach the uncompromised WORD of God from the top of this world, to the bottom, and all the way around. His ministry reaches millions of people worldwide through daily and Sunday TV broadcasts, magazines, teaching audios and videos, conventions and campaigns, and the World Wide Web.

Learn more about Kenneth Copeland Ministries
by visiting our website at **kcm.org**

Believer's Voice of
VICTORY
VICTORY
VICTORY
Whatever
YOU NEED TO
DO
Where Everybody Kno

We're Here for You!®

Your growth in God's WORD and victory in Jesus are at the very center of our hearts. In every way God has equipped us, we will help you deal with the issues facing you, so you can be the **victorious overcomer** He has planned for you to be.

The mission of Kenneth Copeland Ministries is about all of us growing and going together. Our prayer is that you will take full advantage of all The LORD has given us to share with you.

Wherever you are in the world, you can watch the *Believer's Voice of Victory* broadcast on television (check your local listings), the Internet at kcm.org or on our digital Roku channel.

Our website, **kcm.org,** gives you access to every resource we've developed for your victory. And, you can find contact information for our international offices in Africa, Australia, Canada, Europe, Ukraine and our headquarters in the United States.

Each office is staffed with devoted men and women, ready to serve and pray with you. You can contact the worldwide office nearest you for assistance, and you can call us for prayer at our U.S. number, 1-817-852-6000, seven days a week!

We encourage you to connect with us often and let us be part of your everyday walk of faith!

Jesus Is LORD!

Kenneth & Gloria Copeland

Kenneth and Gloria Copeland